Expressive Activities Workbook

Expressive Activities Workbook

Created by Jill Becker

Beyond The Box Doc Publishing
2017

First Printing: 2017

ISBN 978-0-578-19113-3

Beyond The Box Doc Publishing
3 Erie Avenue
Newton, MA 02461

www.beyondtheboxdoc.com

This workbook is dedicated to
my daughter, Becca Rose.
Thank you for choosing me!
ILYMBQU.

Contents

Introduction

Hello and welcome to your Expressive Activities Workbook.

Expressive Arts Therapy is a constellation of modalities which, when used as directives in conjunction with an Expressive Arts Therapist, is a powerful tool through which self-discovery and healing can take place. This workbook includes some of the exercises that my clients have found helpful as we have worked together. Due to the constraints associated with a printed book, this workbook is limited to visual arts and writing exercises. Expressive Arts, however, include music, play, dance, movement, and drama.

When using Expressive Arts Therapy modalities, it is the process, not the product, that is illustrative and healing. Therefore, this workbook cannot, and is in no way meant to, substitute for working with a trained practitioner. Instead, it is meant to be a thought-provoking introduction to some of the Expressive Arts and, hopefully, a starting point from which your own process can evolve.

Before You Begin

This book is designed to be used with various visual arts materials. The following is a suggested list of tools and materials to have on hand as you approach the exercises that are included. Of course, you can add to this list as you desire. Remember, it's *your* process! My one recommendation is that you do not do all of the exercises in one sitting. Instead, spread them out across a few days or weeks.

<u>Your Space</u> I recommend creating a space that is pleasing and calming to you. Consider things like lighting, comfort, temperature and noise levels. Do you like to work in silence or with some background music? Do you prefer to sit on the floor (like I do!) or at a table? Whatever the case, I suggest you make the space somewhere that helps you feel relaxed and at ease. If you have extra space in your home, you might want to consider carving out a place just for you and your process.

<u>Materials</u> Feel free to use whatever materials you prefer. Some suggestions for things to have on hand are listed below. What is most important, however, is that you feel good about the supplies you choose.

- Drawing paper
- Colored Markers
- Colored Pencils
- Graphite Pencil
- Charcoal
- Pastels
- Paints
- Paint Brushes
- Ruler
- Scissors
- Water Container
- Towel

Adding Color to Pages

The act of sitting quietly by yourself or in small groups and adding color to pages can be very meditative. If done mindfully, for example, by paying careful attention to colors, one can experience relaxation and the replenishing of energy. I am starting this activity book with adult coloring pages because I think they are generally less threatening to those of us who don't feel that we are artistic. So, with that, let's begin.

Pre-Activity:
Check in with yourself and your body. Are you finding it difficult to settle in for this activity? Are you experiencing any tension in your body? Take a quick survey of your body and write what you notice below:

Activity:
On the following pages, you will find three images for you to color. After that there is a blank page in case you choose to create both the outline and add the colors.

Consider using colored pencils, markers or paints. Choose whatever materials feel right for you. Become aware of the colors you have available to you. Try and pay attention to the way the paper feels as you add the color to it. Check in with yourself periodically and see how you are feeling. Be aware of any thoughts that come to you as you are working. Remember, this time is for you. Let any thoughts come and go as you enjoy your time.

Post-Activity:

Check in with yourself again. Are you feeling any differently than when you began this activity? Take a quick survey of your body and write what you notice below:

Now go back to the beginning of this activity. Compare what you wrote in the Pre-Activity section with what you just wrote above. Journal about this in the section provided below.

Mandalas

What are Mandalas and why are they included in this book? The word mandala (pronounced mon- dah- lah) means "circle." Tibetan Monks create intricate and beautiful mandalas which exist only for a brief time before they are deconstructed.

As an Expressive Activity, people use mandalas in many ways and for multiple purposes. Oftentimes people enjoy the meditative aspect of putting color on paper and allow themselves time for self-discovery and healing.

The following pages consist of mandalas in various stages of completion. I designed them so that one could move from adding color to designing an entire piece. Of course, you should feel free to use them in any order that speaks to you.

Pre-Activity:
Consider how you feel at this very moment. Are you feeling anxious? Relaxed? Is there anything on your mind? In the space provided, jot down a few words to remind you how you are feeling so you can remember after you are done with your mandala creation.

Activity:
Find a comfortable location. Consider the addition of candles, incense, or music as you look through the pages that follow. Choose one of the printed mandalas or create one of your own.

Allow your senses and feelings to guide your choice of colors and materials.

Consider giving each of your mandalas a date and a title. Every time you engage in this process will likely be different and will reflect who you were at a given time.

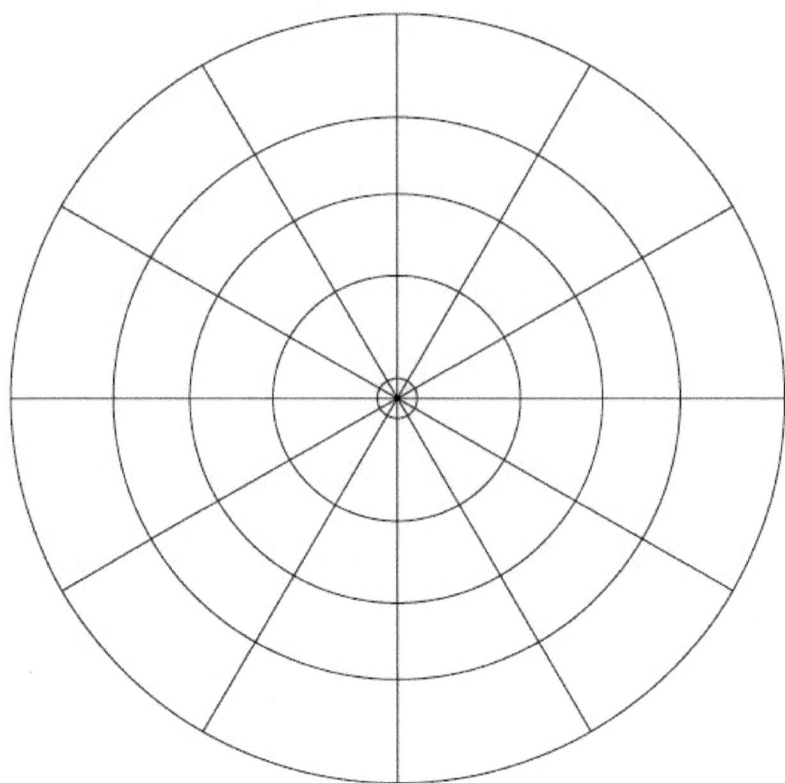

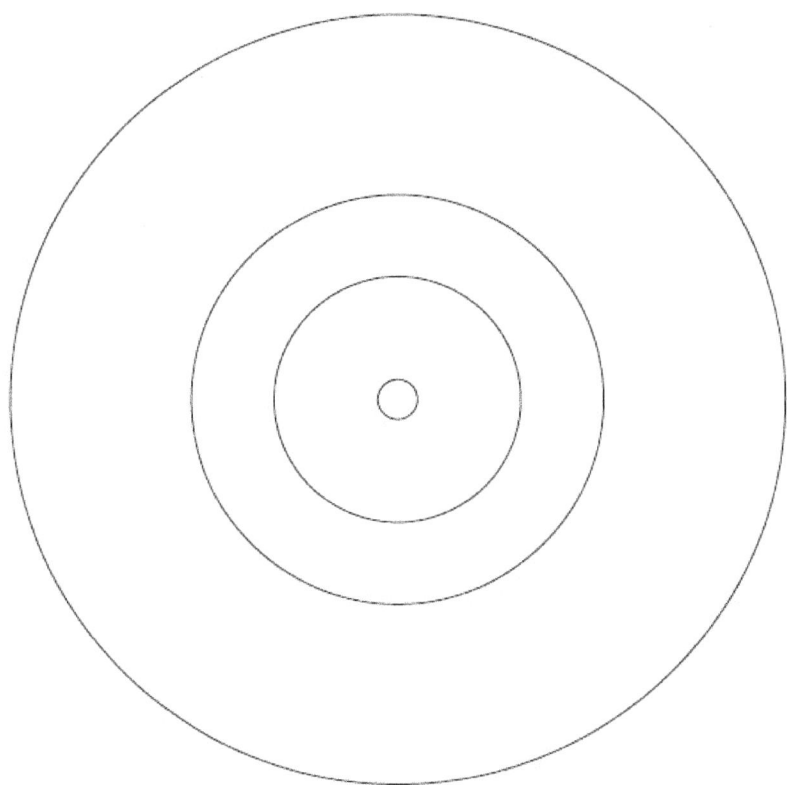

Post-Activity:
How are you now feeling? Are you experiencing any different sensations in your body? How does this compare to before the mandala activity? Take a moment to journal:

Patterned Tiles

Zentangle is a method of achieving a meditative state through drawing simple repeating patterns. I did not create the idea behind Zentangle nor have I studied it extensively. For that reason, I am including what I am calling Patterned Tile drawing here. Whatever you would like to call them, these drawings can be as simple or as complicated as you would like to make them, very few materials are needed, they are self-contained and each can be completed in one sitting. This combined with the fact that so many people like to doodle, made it an ideal item to include in this workbook.

Pre-Activity:
Consider how you are feeling in your mind and in your body. Rate your levels of well-being, stress, anxiety, physical tension or any other measure on a scale from 1-5. Make some notes below:

Well-being

Stress

Anxiety

Physical Tension

Other

Activity:
Choose the tools with which you would like to draw. On the
following blank page, create the outline of a shape that you find
pleasing. A square or a rectangle is the easiest to begin with.
That said, I have been known to outline words and work within
the shapes created by the letters.

Once you have a shape, continue by making lines in order to
divide that shape into sections. Continue dividing the sections
into smaller units until you feel comfortable with the sizes of the
sections you have created.

Now begin making patterns in each of the sections created in
the steps above. I have included an example below since it is
difficult to describe this process using only words. It is included
for illustrative purposes only and is neither right nor wrong.

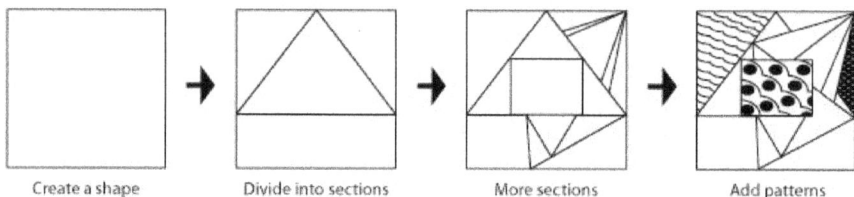

Create a shape	Divide into sections	More sections	Add patterns

Post-Activity:

Now that you have had a chance to work on your own Patterned Tile Drawing, how you are feeling in your mind and in your body. Rate your levels of well-being, stress, anxiety, physical tension or whichever measure you chose at the beginning of this activity. Make some notes below:

Well-being

_____

Stress

_____

Anxiety

_____

Physical Tension

_____

Other

_____

What was that like for you? How did your pre-activity and post activity scales change? When can you envision using this activity? Consider journaling below:

_____

_____

_____

_____

_____

_____

_____

_____

Metaphor

The use of metaphor can help provide comfortable distance from issues in our lives. Metaphors can also help us to focus on what is going well in our lives. This activity is designed to help you focus on the abundance you already have in your life in order to create a positive mindset which, hopefully, will help to increase your sense of health and wellbeing.

Pre-Activity:
Think of some qualities you associate with a tree. List three of them here:

_____

_____

_____

Activity:
On one of the following blank pages, create a tree in an environment. Try not to be self-critical. This activity is about the process, not the product. In fact, the first tree I made looked more like an amoeba than it did a tree! I usually do this exercise with colored pencils. I have a colleague, however, who uses collage. How you approach this is up to you.

As you're working, consider the following parts of the tree. Feel free to label them directly on your drawing if you'd like to. Alternatively, make lists on the back of your piece or on a separate piece of paper.

- Roots: What grounds you?
- Trunk: What gives you support?
- Branches: What goals are you "reaching" for?
- Leaves: What are some things for which you feel gratitude or appreciation?
- Environment: Where is your tree? Is it alone? Is it with other trees?

Post-Activity:
What was that like for you? Did anything surprise you?
Consider journaling about the process below.

Free Write

The next few pages are included for you to continue (or begin!) journaling outside of the activities listed in this book. Journaling can be a wonderful way to process feelings and emotions. Establishing a regular habit of writing daily can help with clarity of thought, as well.

Included below are some journaling prompts. Feel free to use them as you see fit or, if you prefer, ignore them altogether and come up with your own. Remember to check in with yourself before, during, and after the process.

- What almost always brings a smile to my face?
- What inspires me?
- feel most energized when?
- What dreams would I like to come true?
- What would I like to learn?
- What do I have in my life now that I want more (and more) of?
- What does a fun day look like for me - from the moment I wake up to the moment I close my eyes in bed?
- The words I like to live by are:

Mini-Journals

As was discussed in the previous section, journaling is a wonderful way to help process emotion. Sometimes, however, we can't find just the right journal or just the right paper. Other times we want to experience the catharsis associated with journaling but never want to have to read what we wrote. It is for these reasons that I'm including the following method for creating your own mini-journals. Of course, you may find other reasons to use these cute little books.

Pre-Activity:
Consider the following: What types of things do you like to write about? Do you use list-making as a tool in your life? Journaling? What do you do with those lists and journals?

Activity:
Either tear out one of the pages that follow the diagram on the next page or get a fresh sheet of paper. If you choose to use the sheet with the template instead of one of the blank pages, you will also need to cut around the outline of the book in order to have uniformly sized pages.

Some people find following verbal descriptions easier while others prefer images. Both are included on the following page for clarity.

1. Fold along each of the dotted lines as shown on the following page.
2. Fold the whole sheet width-wise.
3. Cut halfway along the center dotted line.
4. Unfold the paper.
5. Fold the sheet length-wise.
6. Push open the center, cut, portion until you see this area form a diamond shape.
7. Fold down all the pages to form a booklet.

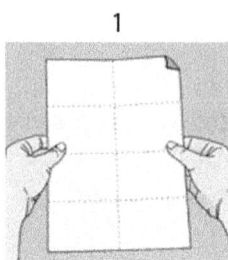

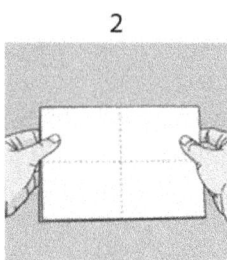

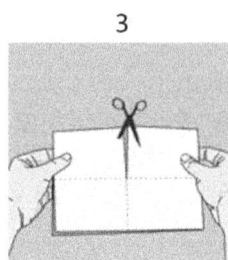

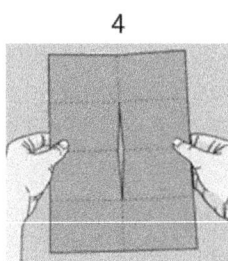

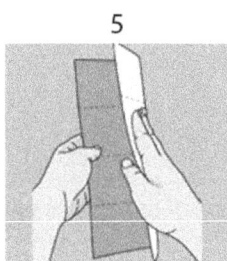

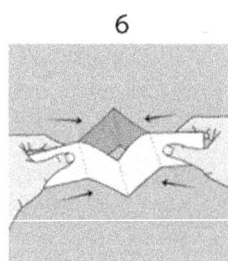

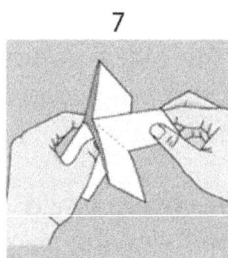

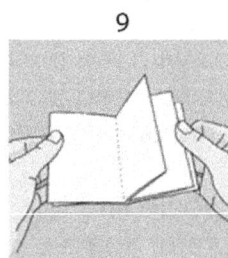

7

8

9

1

5

2

4

3

Post-Activity:

Now that you've had a chance to create your own mini-journals, how will you use them? Did you find this activity useful? Consider writing below:

Mindfulness

Mindfulness is the act of paying attention to something, on purpose. By using mindfulness techniques, we can experience "mini-meditations" throughout our day. I find the use of the senses of the body to be invaluable when attempting to cultivate a mindfulness practice - particularly when my mind is racing and I can't easily slow it down.

Pre-Activity:
Take a survey of your body and your mind. Try and do this systematically so you won't miss any areas of tension or pervasive thoughts. Make note of anything about which you have become aware during this process.

Activity:
Use your senses to direct your focus. Consider each sense in turn and pay attention to what it is telling you. Try and find at least one item for each sense. For example, what are you hearing right now? Certain may be more difficult to pay attention to in this very moment. What is important is being aware and intentionally focusing your mind.

Sight

Hearing

Smell

Touch

Taste

<u>Post-Activity:</u>
Once again, survey your body and your mind. Has anything changed?

_____

_____

_____

_____

What was this experience like for you? Did anything surprise you? How do you feel now?

_____

_____

_____

_____

_____

_____

_____

_____

_____

_____

_____

_____

_____

_____

_____

Personal Crests

Family Crests are symbols on Coats of Arms. Traditionally, the images and colors on these crests all had different meanings. A Personal Crest is something that I developed as I realized that, as individuals, we don't always agree with our family's ideas or values.

Pre-Activity:
What are some of your values? What are some of your strengths? Where do you find your inspiration? Use the area below to brainstorm about qualities that make you uniquely you.

Activity:
Consider items from the brainstorming area above or think of new ones. You will note that the template on the next page is divided into four areas. Decide how you would like to utilize the spaces in each area to create your own Personal Crest.

I have found it helpful to use categories such as values, strengths, gratitude, and work-in-progress when I create my own Personal Crests. At various times I have filled the sections with poetry, words or symbols.

Your Personal Crest is yours. Try to go with your internal flow and see what comes.

Don't forget to give your Personal Crest a title.

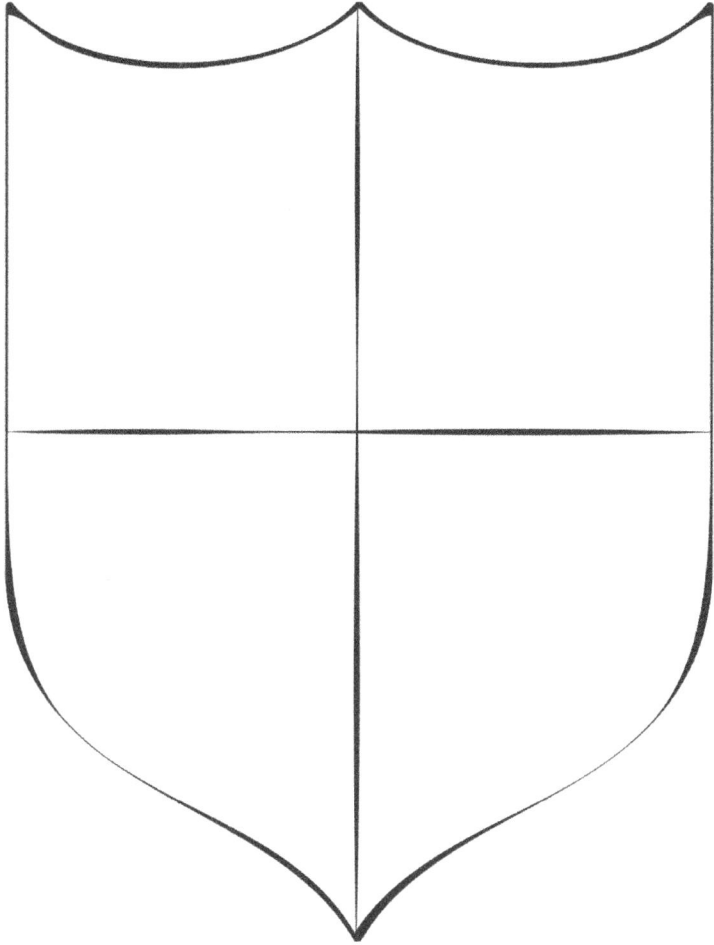

Post-Activity:
How did it feel to make a Personal Crest? Did anything surprise you? How would it have been different if you had been creating a Family Crest? Take a moment to journal:

Thoughts, Notes, Etc.

This section is included for use in any way you might like.
Consider adding images, thoughts, notes, scraps of paper and
anything else you might like.

The Beginning

This section was originally called the "Conclusion." The truth is, however, that each of us can always be in a process of self-discovery. It seemed more fitting, therefore, to call the end-portion of this workbook "The Beginning."

I hope you have found the activities in this book to be thought provoking and a prelude to The Beginning of this portion of your life. I am always interested in feedback. Feel free to be in contact and let me know your thoughts.

With kind regards and warmest wishes for all things wonderful.
~Jill Becker

About Jill

Thank you for the opportunity to introduce myself! Located in Newton, Massachusetts, my unique approach to counseling has developed from my various trainings and my experience with Expressive Arts Therapy. My roles as daughter, friend, partner and mother also inform my interests in mental health, holistic counseling and empowerment. I firmly believe that although we don't always value our strengths, we all have them. By capitalizing on those strengths, we can utilize them as a foundation for healing.

I also believe that the Expressive Arts are accessible to everyone. Even those who do not see themselves as inherently artistic can benefit from the relaxation associated with "doodling" as well as delving deeper under the guidance of a trained professional and via other directives and modalities.

I hope you have enjoyed this workbook. I would like to, once again, stress that this book should not be used as a substitute for working with a trained professional. Instead, it is meant to be a thought provoking introduction to some of the Expressive Arts and, hopefully, a starting point from which your own process can evolve.